PASSWORDS TO LOGIN

THIS BOOK BELONGS TO:

NAME:

PHONE#:

MY EMAIL:

EMERGENCY CONTACT PERSON:

EMERGENGY CONTACT #:

ADDRESS:

OTHER IMPORTANT PEOPLE, PLACES, & THINGS

PASSWORDS TO LOGIN

WEBSITE:
USER ID:
PASSWORD:
EMAIL:
OTHER:

WEBSITE:
USER ID:
PASSWORD:
EMAIL:
OTHER:

WEBSITE:
USER ID:
PASSWORD:
EMAIL:
OTHER:

WEBSITE:
USER ID:
PASSWORD:
EMAIL:
OTHER:

WEBSITE:
USER ID:
PASSWORD:
EMAIL:
OTHER:

WEBSITE:
USER ID:
PASSWORD:
EMAIL:
OTHER:

WEBSITE:
USER ID:
PASSWORD:
EMAIL:
OTHER:

WEBSITE:
USER ID:
PASSWORD:
EMAIL:
OTHER:

PASSWORDS TO LOGIN

WEBSITE:
USER ID:
PASSWORD:
EMAIL:
OTHER:

WEBSITE:
USER ID:
PASSWORD:
EMAIL:
OTHER:

WEBSITE:
USER ID:
PASSWORD:
EMAIL:
OTHER:

WEBSITE:
USER ID:
PASSWORD:
EMAIL:
OTHER:

WEBSITE:
USER ID:
PASSWORD:
EMAIL:
OTHER:

WEBSITE:
USER ID:
PASSWORD:
EMAIL:
OTHER:

WEBSITE:
USER ID:
PASSWORD:
EMAIL:
OTHER:

WEBSITE:
USER ID:
PASSWORD:
EMAIL:
OTHER:

PASSWORDS TO LOGIN

WEBSITE:
USER ID:
PASSWORD:
EMAIL:
OTHER:

WEBSITE:
USER ID:
PASSWORD:
EMAIL:
OTHER:

WEBSITE:
USER ID:
PASSWORD:
EMAIL:
OTHER:

WEBSITE:
USER ID:
PASSWORD:
EMAIL:
OTHER:

WEBSITE:
USER ID:
PASSWORD:
EMAIL:
OTHER:

WEBSITE:
USER ID:
PASSWORD:
EMAIL:
OTHER:

WEBSITE:
USER ID:
PASSWORD:
EMAIL:
OTHER:

WEBSITE:
USER ID:
PASSWORD:
EMAIL:
OTHER:

PASSWORDS TO LOGIN

WEBSITE:
USER ID:
PASSWORD:
EMAIL:
OTHER:

WEBSITE:
USER ID:
PASSWORD:
EMAIL:
OTHER:

WEBSITE:
USER ID:
PASSWORD:
EMAIL:
OTHER:

WEBSITE:
USER ID:
PASSWORD:
EMAIL:
OTHER:

WEBSITE:
USER ID:
PASSWORD:
EMAIL:
OTHER:

WEBSITE:
USER ID:
PASSWORD:
EMAIL:
OTHER:

WEBSITE:
USER ID:
PASSWORD:
EMAIL:
OTHER:

WEBSITE:
USER ID:
PASSWORD:
EMAIL:
OTHER:

PASSWORDS TO LOGIN

WEBSITE:
USER ID:
PASSWORD:
EMAIL:
OTHER:

WEBSITE:
USER ID:
PASSWORD:
EMAIL:
OTHER:

WEBSITE:
USER ID:
PASSWORD:
EMAIL:
OTHER:

WEBSITE:
USER ID:
PASSWORD:
EMAIL:
OTHER:

WEBSITE:
USER ID:
PASSWORD:
EMAIL:
OTHER:

WEBSITE:
USER ID:
PASSWORD:
EMAIL:
OTHER:

WEBSITE:
USER ID:
PASSWORD:
EMAIL:
OTHER:

WEBSITE:
USER ID:
PASSWORD:
EMAIL:
OTHER:

PASSWORDS TO LOGIN

WEBSITE:
USER ID:
PASSWORD:
EMAIL:
OTHER:

WEBSITE:
USER ID:
PASSWORD:
EMAIL:
OTHER:

WEBSITE:
USER ID:
PASSWORD:
EMAIL:
OTHER:

WEBSITE:
USER ID:
PASSWORD:
EMAIL:
OTHER:

WEBSITE:
USER ID:
PASSWORD:
EMAIL:
OTHER:

WEBSITE:
USER ID:
PASSWORD:
EMAIL:
OTHER:

WEBSITE:
USER ID:
PASSWORD:
EMAIL:
OTHER:

WEBSITE:
USER ID:
PASSWORD:
EMAIL:
OTHER:

PASSWORDS TO LOGIN

WEBSITE:
USER ID:
PASSWORD:
EMAIL:
OTHER:

WEBSITE:
USER ID:
PASSWORD:
EMAIL:
OTHER:

WEBSITE:
USER ID:
PASSWORD:
EMAIL:
OTHER:

WEBSITE:
USER ID:
PASSWORD:
EMAIL:
OTHER:

WEBSITE:
USER ID:
PASSWORD:
EMAIL:
OTHER:

WEBSITE:
USER ID:
PASSWORD:
EMAIL:
OTHER:

WEBSITE:
USER ID:
PASSWORD:
EMAIL:
OTHER:

WEBSITE:
USER ID:
PASSWORD:
EMAIL:
OTHER:

PASSWORDS TO LOGIN

WEBSITE:
USER ID:
PASSWORD:
EMAIL:
OTHER:

WEBSITE:
USER ID:
PASSWORD:
EMAIL:
OTHER:

WEBSITE:
USER ID:
PASSWORD:
EMAIL:
OTHER:

WEBSITE:
USER ID:
PASSWORD:
EMAIL:
OTHER:

WEBSITE:
USER ID:
PASSWORD:
EMAIL:
OTHER:

WEBSITE:
USER ID:
PASSWORD:
EMAIL:
OTHER:

WEBSITE:
USER ID:
PASSWORD:
EMAIL:
OTHER:

WEBSITE:
USER ID:
PASSWORD:
EMAIL:
OTHER:

PASSWORDS TO LOGIN

WEBSITE:

USER ID:

PASSWORD:

EMAIL:

OTHER:

WEBSITE:

USER ID:

PASSWORD:

EMAIL:

OTHER:

WEBSITE:

USER ID:

PASSWORD:

EMAIL:

OTHER:

WEBSITE:

USER ID:

PASSWORD:

EMAIL:

OTHER:

WEBSITE:

USER ID:

PASSWORD:

EMAIL:

OTHER:

WEBSITE:

USER ID:

PASSWORD:

EMAIL:

OTHER:

WEBSITE:

USER ID:

PASSWORD:

EMAIL:

OTHER:

WEBSITE:

USER ID:

PASSWORD:

EMAIL:

OTHER:

PASSWORDS TO LOGIN

WEBSITE:
USER ID:
PASSWORD:
EMAIL:
OTHER:

WEBSITE:
USER ID:
PASSWORD:
EMAIL:
OTHER:

WEBSITE:
USER ID:
PASSWORD:
EMAIL:
OTHER:

WEBSITE:
USER ID:
PASSWORD:
EMAIL:
OTHER:

WEBSITE:
USER ID:
PASSWORD:
EMAIL:
OTHER:

WEBSITE:
USER ID:
PASSWORD:
EMAIL:
OTHER:

WEBSITE:
USER ID:
PASSWORD:
EMAIL:
OTHER:

WEBSITE:
USER ID:
PASSWORD:
EMAIL:
OTHER:

WEBSITE:

USER ID:

PASSWORD:

EMAIL:

OTHER:

WEBSITE:

USER ID:

PASSWORD:

EMAIL:

OTHER:

WEBSITE:

USER ID:

PASSWORD:

EMAIL:

OTHER:

WEBSITE:

USER ID:

PASSWORD:

EMAIL:

OTHER:

WEBSITE:

USER ID:

PASSWORD:

EMAIL:

OTHER:

WEBSITE:

USER ID:

PASSWORD:

EMAIL:

OTHER:

WEBSITE:

USER ID:

PASSWORD:

EMAIL:

OTHER:

WEBSITE:

USER ID:

PASSWORD:

EMAIL:

OTHER:

PASSWORDS TO LOGIN

WEBSITE:
USER ID:
PASSWORD:
EMAIL:
OTHER:

WEBSITE:
USER ID:
PASSWORD:
EMAIL:
OTHER:

WEBSITE:
USER ID:
PASSWORD:
EMAIL:
OTHER:

WEBSITE:
USER ID:
PASSWORD:
EMAIL:
OTHER:

WEBSITE:
USER ID:
PASSWORD:
EMAIL:
OTHER:

WEBSITE:
USER ID:
PASSWORD:
EMAIL:
OTHER:

WEBSITE:
USER ID:
PASSWORD:
EMAIL:
OTHER:

WEBSITE:
USER ID:
PASSWORD:
EMAIL:
OTHER:

PASSWORDS TO LOGIN

WEBSITE:
USER ID:
PASSWORD:
EMAIL:
OTHER:

WEBSITE:
USER ID:
PASSWORD:
EMAIL:
OTHER:

WEBSITE:
USER ID:
PASSWORD:
EMAIL:
OTHER:

WEBSITE:
USER ID:
PASSWORD:
EMAIL:
OTHER:

WEBSITE:
USER ID:
PASSWORD:
EMAIL:
OTHER:

WEBSITE:
USER ID:
PASSWORD:
EMAIL:
OTHER:

WEBSITE:
USER ID:
PASSWORD:
EMAIL:
OTHER:

WEBSITE:
USER ID:
PASSWORD:
EMAIL:
OTHER:

PASSWORDS TO LOGIN

WEBSITE:
USER ID:
PASSWORD:
EMAIL:
OTHER:

WEBSITE:
USER ID:
PASSWORD:
EMAIL:
OTHER:

WEBSITE:
USER ID:
PASSWORD:
EMAIL:
OTHER:

WEBSITE:
USER ID:
PASSWORD:
EMAIL:
OTHER:

WEBSITE:
USER ID:
PASSWORD:
EMAIL:
OTHER:

WEBSITE:
USER ID:
PASSWORD:
EMAIL:
OTHER:

WEBSITE:
USER ID:
PASSWORD:
EMAIL:
OTHER:

WEBSITE:
USER ID:
PASSWORD:
EMAIL:
OTHER:

PASSWORDS TO LOGIN

WEBSITE:
USER ID:
PASSWORD:
EMAIL:
OTHER:

WEBSITE:
USER ID:
PASSWORD:
EMAIL:
OTHER:

WEBSITE:
USER ID:
PASSWORD:
EMAIL:
OTHER:

WEBSITE:
USER ID:
PASSWORD:
EMAIL:
OTHER:

WEBSITE:
USER ID:
PASSWORD:
EMAIL:
OTHER:

WEBSITE:
USER ID:
PASSWORD:
EMAIL:
OTHER:

WEBSITE:
USER ID:
PASSWORD:
EMAIL:
OTHER:

WEBSITE:
USER ID:
PASSWORD:
EMAIL:
OTHER:

PASSWORDS TO LOGIN

WEBSITE:
USER ID:
PASSWORD:
EMAIL:
OTHER:

WEBSITE:
USER ID:
PASSWORD:
EMAIL:
OTHER:

WEBSITE:
USER ID:
PASSWORD:
EMAIL:
OTHER:

WEBSITE:
USER ID:
PASSWORD:
EMAIL:
OTHER:

WEBSITE:
USER ID:
PASSWORD:
EMAIL:
OTHER:

WEBSITE:
USER ID:
PASSWORD:
EMAIL:
OTHER:

WEBSITE:
USER ID:
PASSWORD:
EMAIL:
OTHER:

WEBSITE:
USER ID:
PASSWORD:
EMAIL:
OTHER:

PASSWORDS TO LOGIN

WEBSITE:
USER ID:
PASSWORD:
EMAIL:
OTHER:

WEBSITE:
USER ID:
PASSWORD:
EMAIL:
OTHER:

WEBSITE:
USER ID:
PASSWORD:
EMAIL:
OTHER:

WEBSITE:
USER ID:
PASSWORD:
EMAIL:
OTHER:

WEBSITE:
USER ID:
PASSWORD:
EMAIL:
OTHER:

WEBSITE:
USER ID:
PASSWORD:
EMAIL:
OTHER:

WEBSITE:
USER ID:
PASSWORD:
EMAIL:
OTHER:

WEBSITE:
USER ID:
PASSWORD:
EMAIL:
OTHER:

WEBSITE:

USER ID:

PASSWORD:

EMAIL:

OTHER:

WEBSITE:

USER ID:

PASSWORD:

EMAIL:

OTHER:

WEBSITE:

USER ID:

PASSWORD:

EMAIL:

OTHER:

WEBSITE:

USER ID:

PASSWORD:

EMAIL:

OTHER:

WEBSITE:

USER ID:

PASSWORD:

EMAIL:

OTHER:

WEBSITE:

USER ID:

PASSWORD:

EMAIL:

OTHER:

WEBSITE:

USER ID:

PASSWORD:

EMAIL:

OTHER:

WEBSITE:

USER ID:

PASSWORD:

EMAIL:

OTHER:

PASSWORDS TO LOGIN

WEBSITE:
USER ID:
PASSWORD:
EMAIL:
OTHER:

WEBSITE:
USER ID:
PASSWORD:
EMAIL:
OTHER:

WEBSITE:
USER ID:
PASSWORD:
EMAIL:
OTHER:

WEBSITE:
USER ID:
PASSWORD:
EMAIL:
OTHER:

WEBSITE:
USER ID:
PASSWORD:
EMAIL:
OTHER:

WEBSITE:
USER ID:
PASSWORD:
EMAIL:
OTHER:

WEBSITE:
USER ID:
PASSWORD:
EMAIL:
OTHER:

WEBSITE:
USER ID:
PASSWORD:
EMAIL:
OTHER:

PASSWORDS TO LOGIN

WEBSITE:

USER ID:

PASSWORD:

EMAIL:

OTHER:

WEBSITE:

USER ID:

PASSWORD:

EMAIL:

OTHER:

WEBSITE:

USER ID:

PASSWORD:

EMAIL:

OTHER:

WEBSITE:

USER ID:

PASSWORD:

EMAIL:

OTHER:

WEBSITE:

USER ID:

PASSWORD:

EMAIL:

OTHER:

WEBSITE:

USER ID:

PASSWORD:

EMAIL:

OTHER:

WEBSITE:

USER ID:

PASSWORD:

EMAIL:

OTHER:

WEBSITE:

USER ID:

PASSWORD:

EMAIL:

OTHER:

PASSWORDS TO LOGIN

WEBSITE:

USER ID:

PASSWORD:

EMAIL:

OTHER:

WEBSITE:

USER ID:

PASSWORD:

EMAIL:

OTHER:

WEBSITE:

USER ID:

PASSWORD:

EMAIL:

OTHER:

WEBSITE:

USER ID:

PASSWORD:

EMAIL:

OTHER:

WEBSITE:

USER ID:

PASSWORD:

EMAIL:

OTHER:

WEBSITE:

USER ID:

PASSWORD:

EMAIL:

OTHER:

WEBSITE:

USER ID:

PASSWORD:

EMAIL:

OTHER:

WEBSITE:

USER ID:

PASSWORD:

EMAIL:

OTHER:

PASSWORDS TO LOGIN

WEBSITE:

USER ID:

PASSWORD:

EMAIL:

OTHER:

WEBSITE:

USER ID:

PASSWORD:

EMAIL:

OTHER:

WEBSITE:

USER ID:

PASSWORD:

EMAIL:

OTHER:

WEBSITE:

USER ID:

PASSWORD:

EMAIL:

OTHER:

WEBSITE:

USER ID:

PASSWORD:

EMAIL:

OTHER:

WEBSITE:

USER ID:

PASSWORD:

EMAIL:

OTHER:

WEBSITE:

USER ID:

PASSWORD:

EMAIL:

OTHER:

WEBSITE:

USER ID:

PASSWORD:

EMAIL:

OTHER:

PASSWORDS TO LOGIN

WEBSITE:
USER ID:
PASSWORD:
EMAIL:
OTHER:

WEBSITE:
USER ID:
PASSWORD:
EMAIL:
OTHER:

WEBSITE:
USER ID:
PASSWORD:
EMAIL:
OTHER:

WEBSITE:
USER ID:
PASSWORD:
EMAIL:
OTHER:

WEBSITE:
USER ID:
PASSWORD:
EMAIL:
OTHER:

WEBSITE:
USER ID:
PASSWORD:
EMAIL:
OTHER:

WEBSITE:
USER ID:
PASSWORD:
EMAIL:
OTHER:

WEBSITE:
USER ID:
PASSWORD:
EMAIL:
OTHER:

PASSWORDS TO LOGIN

WEBSITE:
USER ID:
PASSWORD:
EMAIL:
OTHER:

WEBSITE:
USER ID:
PASSWORD:
EMAIL:
OTHER:

WEBSITE:
USER ID:
PASSWORD:
EMAIL:
OTHER:

WEBSITE:
USER ID:
PASSWORD:
EMAIL:
OTHER:

WEBSITE:
USER ID:
PASSWORD:
EMAIL:
OTHER:

WEBSITE:
USER ID:
PASSWORD:
EMAIL:
OTHER:

WEBSITE:
USER ID:
PASSWORD:
EMAIL:
OTHER:

WEBSITE:
USER ID:
PASSWORD:
EMAIL:
OTHER:

PASSWORDS TO LOGIN

WEBSITE:
USER ID:
PASSWORD:
EMAIL:
OTHER:

WEBSITE:
USER ID:
PASSWORD:
EMAIL:
OTHER:

WEBSITE:
USER ID:
PASSWORD:
EMAIL:
OTHER:

WEBSITE:
USER ID:
PASSWORD:
EMAIL:
OTHER:

WEBSITE:
USER ID:
PASSWORD:
EMAIL:
OTHER:

WEBSITE:
USER ID:
PASSWORD:
EMAIL:
OTHER:

WEBSITE:
USER ID:
PASSWORD:
EMAIL:
OTHER:

WEBSITE:
USER ID:
PASSWORD:
EMAIL:
OTHER:

PASSWORDS TO LOGIN

WEBSITE:
USER ID:
PASSWORD:
EMAIL:
OTHER:

WEBSITE:
USER ID:
PASSWORD:
EMAIL:
OTHER:

WEBSITE:
USER ID:
PASSWORD:
EMAIL:
OTHER:

WEBSITE:
USER ID:
PASSWORD:
EMAIL:
OTHER:

WEBSITE:
USER ID:
PASSWORD:
EMAIL:
OTHER:

WEBSITE:
USER ID:
PASSWORD:
EMAIL:
OTHER:

WEBSITE:
USER ID:
PASSWORD:
EMAIL:
OTHER:

WEBSITE:
USER ID:
PASSWORD:
EMAIL:
OTHER:

PASSWORDS TO LOGIN

WEBSITE:

USER ID:

PASSWORD:

EMAIL:

OTHER:

WEBSITE:

USER ID:

PASSWORD:

EMAIL:

OTHER:

WEBSITE:

USER ID:

PASSWORD:

EMAIL:

OTHER:

WEBSITE:

USER ID:

PASSWORD:

EMAIL:

OTHER:

WEBSITE:

USER ID:

PASSWORD:

EMAIL:

OTHER:

WEBSITE:

USER ID:

PASSWORD:

EMAIL:

OTHER:

WEBSITE:

USER ID:

PASSWORD:

EMAIL:

OTHER:

WEBSITE:

USER ID:

PASSWORD:

EMAIL:

OTHER:

PASSWORDS TO LOGIN

WEBSITE:
USER ID:
PASSWORD:
EMAIL:
OTHER:

WEBSITE:
USER ID:
PASSWORD:
EMAIL:
OTHER:

WEBSITE:
USER ID:
PASSWORD:
EMAIL:
OTHER:

WEBSITE:
USER ID:
PASSWORD:
EMAIL:
OTHER:

WEBSITE:
USER ID:
PASSWORD:
EMAIL:
OTHER:

WEBSITE:
USER ID:
PASSWORD:
EMAIL:
OTHER:

WEBSITE:
USER ID:
PASSWORD:
EMAIL:
OTHER:

WEBSITE:
USER ID:
PASSWORD:
EMAIL:
OTHER:

PASSWORDS TO LOGIN

WEBSITE:
USER ID:
PASSWORD:
EMAIL:
OTHER:

WEBSITE:
USER ID:
PASSWORD:
EMAIL:
OTHER:

WEBSITE:
USER ID:
PASSWORD:
EMAIL:
OTHER:

WEBSITE:
USER ID:
PASSWORD:
EMAIL:
OTHER:

WEBSITE:
USER ID:
PASSWORD:
EMAIL:
OTHER:

WEBSITE:
USER ID:
PASSWORD:
EMAIL:
OTHER:

WEBSITE:
USER ID:
PASSWORD:
EMAIL:
OTHER:

WEBSITE:
USER ID:
PASSWORD:
EMAIL:
OTHER:

PASSWORDS TO LOGIN

WEBSITE:
USER ID:
PASSWORD:
EMAIL:
OTHER:

WEBSITE:
USER ID:
PASSWORD:
EMAIL:
OTHER:

WEBSITE:
USER ID:
PASSWORD:
EMAIL:
OTHER:

WEBSITE:
USER ID:
PASSWORD:
EMAIL:
OTHER:

WEBSITE:
USER ID:
PASSWORD:
EMAIL:
OTHER:

WEBSITE:
USER ID:
PASSWORD:
EMAIL:
OTHER:

WEBSITE:
USER ID:
PASSWORD:
EMAIL:
OTHER:

WEBSITE:
USER ID:
PASSWORD:
EMAIL:
OTHER:

PASSWORDS TO LOGIN

WEBSITE:
USER ID:
PASSWORD:
EMAIL:
OTHER:

WEBSITE:
USER ID:
PASSWORD:
EMAIL:
OTHER:

WEBSITE:
USER ID:
PASSWORD:
EMAIL:
OTHER:

WEBSITE:
USER ID:
PASSWORD:
EMAIL:
OTHER:

WEBSITE:
USER ID:
PASSWORD:
EMAIL:
OTHER:

WEBSITE:
USER ID:
PASSWORD:
EMAIL:
OTHER:

WEBSITE:
USER ID:
PASSWORD:
EMAIL:
OTHER:

WEBSITE:
USER ID:
PASSWORD:
EMAIL:
OTHER:

PASSWORDS TO LOGIN

WEBSITE:
USER ID:
PASSWORD:
EMAIL:
OTHER:

WEBSITE:
USER ID:
PASSWORD:
EMAIL:
OTHER:

WEBSITE:
USER ID:
PASSWORD:
EMAIL:
OTHER:

WEBSITE:
USER ID:
PASSWORD:
EMAIL:
OTHER:

WEBSITE:
USER ID:
PASSWORD:
EMAIL:
OTHER:

WEBSITE:
USER ID:
PASSWORD:
EMAIL:
OTHER:

WEBSITE:
USER ID:
PASSWORD:
EMAIL:
OTHER:

WEBSITE:
USER ID:
PASSWORD:
EMAIL:
OTHER:

PASSWORDS TO LOGIN

WEBSITE:
USER ID:
PASSWORD:
EMAIL:
OTHER:

WEBSITE:
USER ID:
PASSWORD:
EMAIL:
OTHER:

WEBSITE:
USER ID:
PASSWORD:
EMAIL:
OTHER:

WEBSITE:
USER ID:
PASSWORD:
EMAIL:
OTHER:

WEBSITE:
USER ID:
PASSWORD:
EMAIL:
OTHER:

WEBSITE:
USER ID:
PASSWORD:
EMAIL:
OTHER:

WEBSITE:
USER ID:
PASSWORD:
EMAIL:
OTHER:

WEBSITE:
USER ID:
PASSWORD:
EMAIL:
OTHER:

PASSWORDS TO LOGIN

WEBSITE:
USER ID:
PASSWORD:
EMAIL:
OTHER:

WEBSITE:
USER ID:
PASSWORD:
EMAIL:
OTHER:

WEBSITE:
USER ID:
PASSWORD:
EMAIL:
OTHER:

WEBSITE:
USER ID:
PASSWORD:
EMAIL:
OTHER:

WEBSITE:
USER ID:
PASSWORD:
EMAIL:
OTHER:

WEBSITE:
USER ID:
PASSWORD:
EMAIL:
OTHER:

WEBSITE:
USER ID:
PASSWORD:
EMAIL:
OTHER:

WEBSITE:
USER ID:
PASSWORD:
EMAIL:
OTHER:

PASSWORDS TO LOGIN

WEBSITE:
USER ID:
PASSWORD:
EMAIL:
OTHER:

WEBSITE:
USER ID:
PASSWORD:
EMAIL:
OTHER:

WEBSITE:
USER ID:
PASSWORD:
EMAIL:
OTHER:

WEBSITE:
USER ID:
PASSWORD:
EMAIL:
OTHER:

WEBSITE:
USER ID:
PASSWORD:
EMAIL:
OTHER:

WEBSITE:
USER ID:
PASSWORD:
EMAIL:
OTHER:

WEBSITE:
USER ID:
PASSWORD:
EMAIL:
OTHER:

WEBSITE:
USER ID:
PASSWORD:
EMAIL:
OTHER:

PASSWORDS TO LOGIN

WEBSITE:
USER ID:
PASSWORD:
EMAIL:
OTHER:

WEBSITE:
USER ID:
PASSWORD:
EMAIL:
OTHER:

WEBSITE:
USER ID:
PASSWORD:
EMAIL:
OTHER:

WEBSITE:
USER ID:
PASSWORD:
EMAIL:
OTHER:

WEBSITE:
USER ID:
PASSWORD:
EMAIL:
OTHER:

WEBSITE:
USER ID:
PASSWORD:
EMAIL:
OTHER:

WEBSITE:
USER ID:
PASSWORD:
EMAIL:
OTHER:

WEBSITE:
USER ID:
PASSWORD:
EMAIL:
OTHER:

PASSWORDS TO LOGIN

WEBSITE:
USER ID:
PASSWORD:
EMAIL:
OTHER:

WEBSITE:
USER ID:
PASSWORD:
EMAIL:
OTHER:

WEBSITE:
USER ID:
PASSWORD:
EMAIL:
OTHER:

WEBSITE:
USER ID:
PASSWORD:
EMAIL:
OTHER:

WEBSITE:
USER ID:
PASSWORD:
EMAIL:
OTHER:

WEBSITE:
USER ID:
PASSWORD:
EMAIL:
OTHER:

WEBSITE:
USER ID:
PASSWORD:
EMAIL:
OTHER:

WEBSITE:
USER ID:
PASSWORD:
EMAIL:
OTHER:

PASSWORDS TO LOGIN

WEBSITE:
USER ID:
PASSWORD:
EMAIL:
OTHER:

WEBSITE:
USER ID:
PASSWORD:
EMAIL:
OTHER:

WEBSITE:
USER ID:
PASSWORD:
EMAIL:
OTHER:

WEBSITE:
USER ID:
PASSWORD:
EMAIL:
OTHER:

WEBSITE:
USER ID:
PASSWORD:
EMAIL:
OTHER:

WEBSITE:
USER ID:
PASSWORD:
EMAIL:
OTHER:

WEBSITE:
USER ID:
PASSWORD:
EMAIL:
OTHER:

WEBSITE:
USER ID:
PASSWORD:
EMAIL:
OTHER:

PASSWORDS TO LOGIN

WEBSITE:
USER ID:
PASSWORD:
EMAIL:
OTHER:

WEBSITE:
USER ID:
PASSWORD:
EMAIL:
OTHER:

WEBSITE:
USER ID:
PASSWORD:
EMAIL:
OTHER:

WEBSITE:
USER ID:
PASSWORD:
EMAIL:
OTHER:

WEBSITE:
USER ID:
PASSWORD:
EMAIL:
OTHER:

WEBSITE:
USER ID:
PASSWORD:
EMAIL:
OTHER:

WEBSITE:
USER ID:
PASSWORD:
EMAIL:
OTHER:

WEBSITE:
USER ID:
PASSWORD:
EMAIL:
OTHER:

PASSWORDS TO LOGIN

WEBSITE:
USER ID:
PASSWORD:
EMAIL:
OTHER:

WEBSITE:
USER ID:
PASSWORD:
EMAIL:
OTHER:

WEBSITE:
USER ID:
PASSWORD:
EMAIL:
OTHER:

WEBSITE:
USER ID:
PASSWORD:
EMAIL:
OTHER:

WEBSITE:
USER ID:
PASSWORD:
EMAIL:
OTHER:

WEBSITE:
USER ID:
PASSWORD:
EMAIL:
OTHER:

WEBSITE:
USER ID:
PASSWORD:
EMAIL:
OTHER:

WEBSITE:
USER ID:
PASSWORD:
EMAIL:
OTHER:

PASSWORDS TO LOGIN

WEBSITE:
USER ID:
PASSWORD:
EMAIL:
OTHER:

WEBSITE:
USER ID:
PASSWORD:
EMAIL:
OTHER:

WEBSITE:
USER ID:
PASSWORD:
EMAIL:
OTHER:

WEBSITE:
USER ID:
PASSWORD:
EMAIL:
OTHER:

WEBSITE:
USER ID:
PASSWORD:
EMAIL:
OTHER:

WEBSITE:
USER ID:
PASSWORD:
EMAIL:
OTHER:

WEBSITE:
USER ID:
PASSWORD:
EMAIL:
OTHER:

WEBSITE:
USER ID:
PASSWORD:
EMAIL:
OTHER:

PASSWORDS TO LOGIN

WEBSITE:

USER ID:

PASSWORD:

EMAIL:

OTHER:

WEBSITE:

USER ID:

PASSWORD:

EMAIL:

OTHER:

WEBSITE:

USER ID:

PASSWORD:

EMAIL:

OTHER:

WEBSITE:

USER ID:

PASSWORD:

EMAIL:

OTHER:

WEBSITE:

USER ID:

PASSWORD:

EMAIL:

OTHER:

WEBSITE:

USER ID:

PASSWORD:

EMAIL:

OTHER:

WEBSITE:

USER ID:

PASSWORD:

EMAIL:

OTHER:

WEBSITE:

USER ID:

PASSWORD:

EMAIL:

OTHER:

PASSWORDS TO LOGIN

WEBSITE:
USER ID:
PASSWORD:
EMAIL:
OTHER:

WEBSITE:
USER ID:
PASSWORD:
EMAIL:
OTHER:

WEBSITE:
USER ID:
PASSWORD:
EMAIL:
OTHER:

WEBSITE:
USER ID:
PASSWORD:
EMAIL:
OTHER:

WEBSITE:
USER ID:
PASSWORD:
EMAIL:
OTHER:

WEBSITE:
USER ID:
PASSWORD:
EMAIL:
OTHER:

WEBSITE:
USER ID:
PASSWORD:
EMAIL:
OTHER:

WEBSITE:
USER ID:
PASSWORD:
EMAIL:
OTHER:

PASSWORDS TO LOGIN

WEBSITE:
USER ID:
PASSWORD:
EMAIL:
OTHER:

WEBSITE:
USER ID:
PASSWORD:
EMAIL:
OTHER:

WEBSITE:
USER ID:
PASSWORD:
EMAIL:
OTHER:

WEBSITE:
USER ID:
PASSWORD:
EMAIL:
OTHER:

WEBSITE:
USER ID:
PASSWORD:
EMAIL:
OTHER:

WEBSITE:
USER ID:
PASSWORD:
EMAIL:
OTHER:

WEBSITE:
USER ID:
PASSWORD:
EMAIL:
OTHER:

WEBSITE:
USER ID:
PASSWORD:
EMAIL:
OTHER:

PASSWORDS TO LOGIN

WEBSITE:
USER ID:
PASSWORD:
EMAIL:
OTHER:

WEBSITE:
USER ID:
PASSWORD:
EMAIL:
OTHER:

WEBSITE:
USER ID:
PASSWORD:
EMAIL:
OTHER:

WEBSITE:
USER ID:
PASSWORD:
EMAIL:
OTHER:

WEBSITE:
USER ID:
PASSWORD:
EMAIL:
OTHER:

WEBSITE:
USER ID:
PASSWORD:
EMAIL:
OTHER:

WEBSITE:
USER ID:
PASSWORD:
EMAIL:
OTHER:

WEBSITE:
USER ID:
PASSWORD:
EMAIL:
OTHER:

PASSWORDS TO LOGIN

WEBSITE:
USER ID:
PASSWORD:
EMAIL:
OTHER:

WEBSITE:
USER ID:
PASSWORD:
EMAIL:
OTHER:

WEBSITE:
USER ID:
PASSWORD:
EMAIL:
OTHER:

WEBSITE:
USER ID:
PASSWORD:
EMAIL:
OTHER:

WEBSITE:
USER ID:
PASSWORD:
EMAIL:
OTHER:

WEBSITE:
USER ID:
PASSWORD:
EMAIL:
OTHER:

WEBSITE:
USER ID:
PASSWORD:
EMAIL:
OTHER:

WEBSITE:
USER ID:
PASSWORD:
EMAIL:
OTHER:

PASSWORDS TO LOGIN

WEBSITE:

USER ID:

PASSWORD:

EMAIL:

OTHER:

WEBSITE:

USER ID:

PASSWORD:

EMAIL:

OTHER:

WEBSITE:

USER ID:

PASSWORD:

EMAIL:

OTHER:

WEBSITE:

USER ID:

PASSWORD:

EMAIL:

OTHER:

WEBSITE:

USER ID:

PASSWORD:

EMAIL:

OTHER:

WEBSITE:

USER ID:

PASSWORD:

EMAIL:

OTHER:

WEBSITE:

USER ID:

PASSWORD:

EMAIL:

OTHER:

WEBSITE:

USER ID:

PASSWORD:

EMAIL:

OTHER:

PASSWORDS TO LOGIN

WEBSITE:
USER ID:
PASSWORD:
EMAIL:
OTHER:

WEBSITE:
USER ID:
PASSWORD:
EMAIL:
OTHER:

WEBSITE:
USER ID:
PASSWORD:
EMAIL:
OTHER:

WEBSITE:
USER ID:
PASSWORD:
EMAIL:
OTHER:

WEBSITE:
USER ID:
PASSWORD:
EMAIL:
OTHER:

WEBSITE:
USER ID:
PASSWORD:
EMAIL:
OTHER:

WEBSITE:
USER ID:
PASSWORD:
EMAIL:
OTHER:

WEBSITE:
USER ID:
PASSWORD:
EMAIL:
OTHER:

PASSWORDS TO LOGIN

WEBSITE:
USER ID:
PASSWORD:
EMAIL:
OTHER:

WEBSITE:
USER ID:
PASSWORD:
EMAIL:
OTHER:

WEBSITE:
USER ID:
PASSWORD:
EMAIL:
OTHER:

WEBSITE:
USER ID:
PASSWORD:
EMAIL:
OTHER:

WEBSITE:
USER ID:
PASSWORD:
EMAIL:
OTHER:

WEBSITE:
USER ID:
PASSWORD:
EMAIL:
OTHER:

WEBSITE:
USER ID:
PASSWORD:
EMAIL:
OTHER:

WEBSITE:
USER ID:
PASSWORD:
EMAIL:
OTHER:

PASSWORDS TO LOGIN

WEBSITE:
USER ID:
PASSWORD:
EMAIL:
OTHER:

WEBSITE:
USER ID:
PASSWORD:
EMAIL:
OTHER:

WEBSITE:
USER ID:
PASSWORD:
EMAIL:
OTHER:

WEBSITE:
USER ID:
PASSWORD:
EMAIL:
OTHER:

WEBSITE:
USER ID:
PASSWORD:
EMAIL:
OTHER:

WEBSITE:
USER ID:
PASSWORD:
EMAIL:
OTHER:

WEBSITE:
USER ID:
PASSWORD:
EMAIL:
OTHER:

WEBSITE:
USER ID:
PASSWORD:
EMAIL:
OTHER:

Made in the USA
Monee, IL
05 November 2026

67380851R00031